STEM ADVENTURES

SENSATIONAL SCIENCE

First edition for the United States and
Canada published in 2018
by Barron's Educational Series, Inc.

All inquiries should be addressed to:
Barron's Educational Series, Inc.
250 Wireless Boulevard
Hauppauge, NY 11788
www.barronseduc.com

ISBN: 978-1-4380-1251-3

Date of Manufacture: July 2018
Manufactured by: RRD Asia, Dongguan, China

Printed in China
9 8 7 6 5 4 3 2 1

Executive editor: Bryony Davies
Design: Kate Wiliwinska
Designed and packaged by: The Shop
Illustrated by: Dynamo Limited
Picture research: Steve Behan and Paul Langan
Production: Nicola Davey

AUTHOR:

STEPHANIE CLARKSON is a writer and
journalist and has been writing for children for the past
decade. Her experience allows her to excel at making
complex subject areas accessible to young readers,
and she has penned educational and nonfiction titles for
leading trade publishers on current affairs, technology,
art, travel, and mental health.

STEM EDITORIAL CONSULTANT:

MARGARET (MEG) KÄUFER is a
founding member and current president of the STEM
Alliance of Larchmont-Mamaroneck, NY. The STEM
Alliance is a nonprofit organization with the mission of
creating a network of STEM learning opportunities to
connect today's youth to the jobs of the future. They work
closely with local schools to run hands-on, applied STEM
enrichment experiences. Highlights of their work under
her leadership include launching an annual public STEM
festival, establishing competitive robotics teams, and
creating a hands-on STEM summer enrichment program
for at-risk children. Meg has her Masters in Curriculum &
Instruction from Teachers College, Columbia University.
Throughout her career, Meg has championed STEM
learning for its capacity to engage and inspire all
varieties of learners.

PICTURE ACKNOWLEDGMENTS

The publishers would like to thank the following sources for their kind
permission to reproduce the pictures in the book.

Pages 6–7: Alexandr III/Shutterstock; 9 (top right) Public Domain; 12
(bottom left) Juan Gaertner/Shutterstock; 17 (top right) NASA; 18
(bottom left) Manzrussali/Shutterstock; 20 (left) Library of Congress;
22 (top right) Public Domain, (bottom right) Chinasong/Shutterstock;
23 (bottom right) Boonchuay Promjiam/Shutterstock; 24 (top) Serega
K Photo and Video/Shutterstock; 25 (bottom) VanderWolf Images/
Shutterstock; 26 (top right) Library of Congress; 27 (bottom) Photobank
Gallery/Shutterstock; 29 (top right) Ivan Lukyanchuk/Shutterstock;
30 (left) Georgios Kollidas/Shutterstock; 31 (top right) Macrovector/
Shutterstock; 32 (left) Titov Nikolai/Shutterstock; 34 (top left) Photobort/
Shutterstock, (top right) David Ryo/Shutterstock, (left) Antonio Truzzi/
Shutterstock, (right) Lars Hallstrom/Shutterstock, (bottom left)
MLArduengo/Shutterstock, (bottom right) Paul Wishart/Shutterstock;
35 (top) CERN Photo Lab; 38 (key) Aboikis/Shutterstock, (log)
FotograFF/Shutterstock, (cat) Hannadarzy/Shutterstock, (egg) Vankad/
Shutterstock; 40 (top) SlayStorm/Shutterstock; 41 (top) Sumire8/
Shutterstock; 43 (top) Bess Hamitii/Shutterstock; 44 (top) Guten Tag
Vector/Shutterstock; 45 (humpback whale) Tomas Kotouc/Shutterstock,
(shark) Zebra0209/Shutterstock, (spider web) SJ Travel Photo and
Video/Shutterstock, (butterfly wings) Jps/Shutterstock, (burrs) Jackan/
Shutterstock, (kingfisher) Rudmer Zwerver/Shutterstock, (tablet)
Lucadp/Shutterstock, (velcro) Daniel Brasil/Shutterstock, (wind turbine)
Diyanski/Shutterstock, (train) Wayne0216/Shutterstock, (swimming
costume) XiXinXing/Shutterstock, (tape) Kwangmoozaa/Shutterstock;
46 (bottom right) La Gorda/Shutterstock; 47 (top right) Chokniti
Khongchum/Shutterstock; 49 (center) Studio concept/Shutterstock,
(bottom left) Mark Nazh/Shutterstock; 50 (left) Universal History
Archive/UIG/Getty Images; 51 (top right) Rudmer Zwerver/Shutterstock;
52 (bottom left) Monet_3k/Shutterstock, (bottom center) Public Domain,
(bottom right) Dave Guttridge/Imperial College London; 57 (center)
Natural History Museum of Utah; 59 (top right) Sakdinon Kadchiangsaen/
Shutterstock; 60 (top right) Shawn Hempel/Shutterstock, (bottom)
AllNikart/Shutterstock

Every effort has been made to acknowledge correctly and
contact the source and/or copyright holder of each picture,
and Carlton Books apologizes for any unintentional
errors or omissions, which will be corrected in
future editions of this book.

STEM ADVENTURES

SENSATIONAL
SCIENCE

Stephanie Clarkson

BARRON'S

CONTENTS

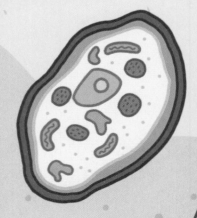

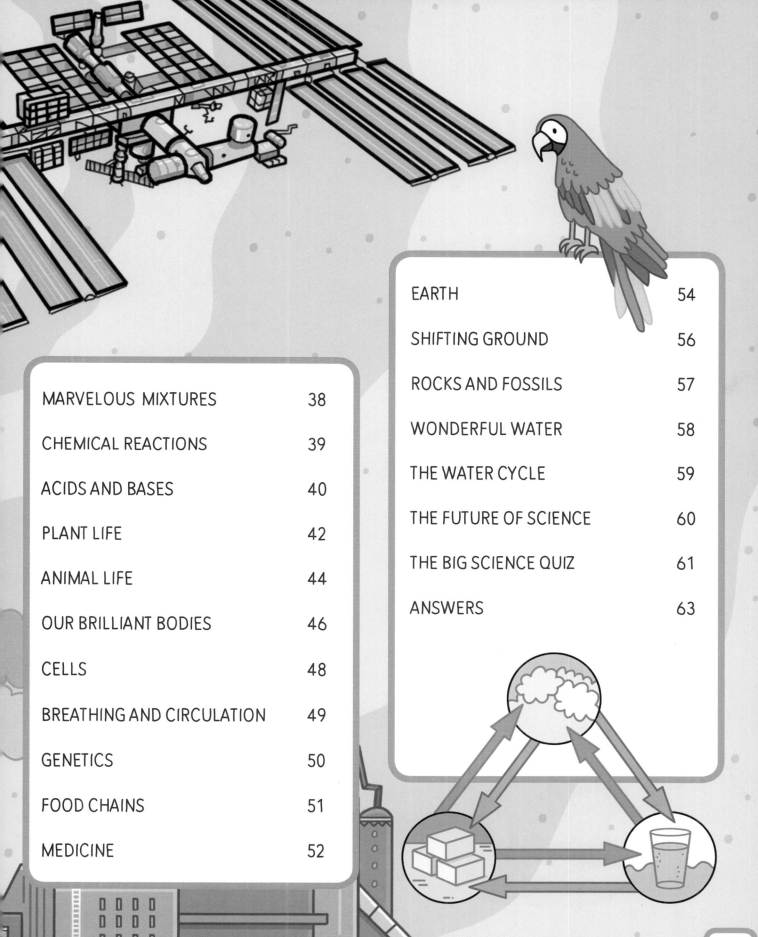

SUPER STEM

Welcome to the world of STEM. STEM stands for science, technology, engineering, and math. These four fabulous subjects open up a world of exciting discovery.

You probably already possess many of the qualities and interests shared by great scientists, technologists, engineers, and mathematicians. Read each statement and put a check in the box if it applies to you.

SCIENCE

YOU...

- are curious about the world around you. ☐

- love to ask questions. ☐

- experiment and try new things, even if it means making a mistake. ☐

You're already on your way to becoming a scientist! You're excited to discover more about the way scientists think and work.

TECHNOLOGY

YOU...

- are always playing with gadgets. ☐

- like to understand exactly how machines work. ☐

- try to find ways of making everyday tasks easier, such as investigating whether a different route to school makes the trip shorter. ☐

Technology is right up your alley! You're fascinated by the latest products and want to find out more about inventions that help improve our world.

ENGINEERING

YOU...

- like using your brain to solve problems. ❑

- love playing with construction sets and building blocks. ❑

- enjoy building amazing dens or dams in streams. ❑

You're perfectly suited to a career as an engineer! You could invent or make amazing tools, machines, and buildings.

MATH

YOU...

- like to understand the reasons why something is true. ❑

- often spot patterns in pictures and clothing or sequences in numbers like football statistics. ❑

- love 3-D puzzles, card games, and logic games like chess. ❑

You're a born mathematician! You're excited by shapes and measurements and curious to see what numbers can do when you use them in different ways.

WHAT IS SCIENCE?

This book is all about science. Science is our way of finding answers to the mysteries of life. Scientists want to help improve our understanding of the history of the world and how our universe works. Scientists ask questions about the world around them, make predictions, test those theories, and then organize and share their knowledge.

There are still many mysteries scientists are working to solve. Perhaps one day you will help find out how our brains work, or you will answer age-old questions such as, "Why does gravity only pull?" You might even use hands-on science to solve problems, such as how to make biodegradable plastic or how to prove if there is alien life in our universe. Science is all around us!

FIELDS OF SCIENCE

Scientists can study anything from the tiniest microorganism to vast areas of outer space. There are many different areas of science. Each one can help us answer questions and improve our understanding of the world around us.

ACTIVITY

Can you draw an arrow to match each branch of science to the correct explanation? The first one has been done for you.

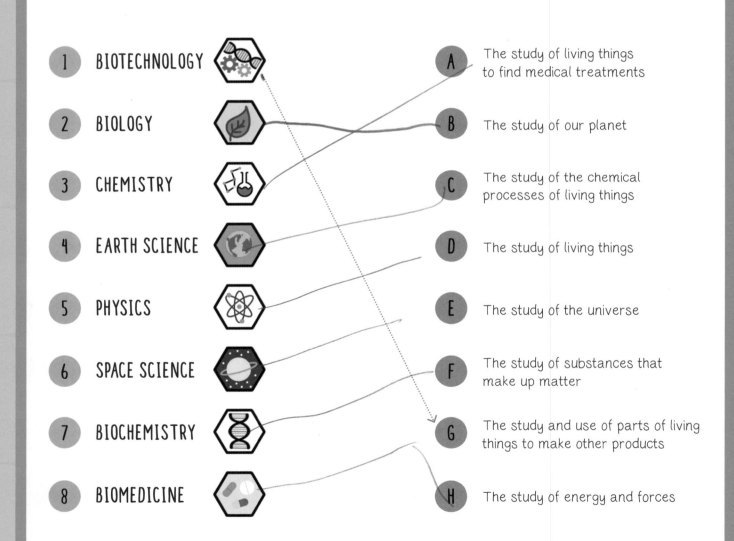

1. BIOTECHNOLOGY
2. BIOLOGY
3. CHEMISTRY
4. EARTH SCIENCE
5. PHYSICS
6. SPACE SCIENCE
7. BIOCHEMISTRY
8. BIOMEDICINE

A. The study of living things to find medical treatments
B. The study of our planet
C. The study of the chemical processes of living things
D. The study of living things
E. The study of the universe
F. The study of substances that make up matter
G. The study and use of parts of living things to make other products
H. The study of energy and forces

THE HISTORY OF SCIENCE

In ancient times, people made up stories to explain things they couldn't understand. Things started to change about 2,500 years ago when Greek thinkers began to question the workings of the universe by looking at the natural world around them.

ARCHIMEDES

Archimedes lived in Sicily, Italy between 287 and 212 B.C.E. One day he noticed that some water spilled over the edge of his bathtub as he got in. As a result, he came up with a brand new principle to explain whether an object floats or sinks.

ACTIVITY

Archimedes' principle, the law of buoyancy, is still used today. It describes how ships float. Crack the code to discover what Archimedes said when he made his big discovery.

CODE KEY

A	B	C	D	E	F	G
?	$	9	\	7	~	4

H	I	J	K	L	M	N
6	&	^	+	8	=	(

O	P	Q	R	S	T	U
3	/	1	%	*	}	@

V	W	X	Y	Z
)	!	5	-	2

7	@	%	7	+	?

THINK LIKE A SCIENTIST

Modern scientists use a special method to help them work. First they ask a question. Next, they conduct research by gathering information on the subject, and then they form a hypothesis (a prediction). They then test their hypothesis with experiments and record their results.

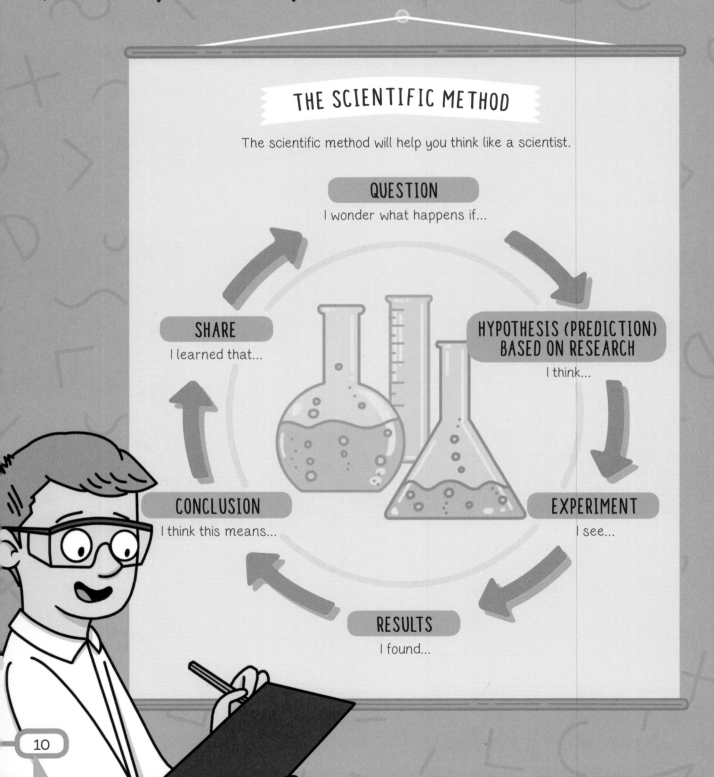

THE SCIENTIFIC METHOD

The scientific method will help you think like a scientist.

QUESTION
I wonder what happens if...

HYPOTHESIS (PREDICTION) BASED ON RESEARCH
I think...

EXPERIMENT
I see...

RESULTS
I found...

CONCLUSION
I think this means...

SHARE
I learned that...

Scientists come up with lots of interesting theories about the world and how it works, but a theory can't be accepted until it has been properly tested. Scientists use results to repeat and test past experiments and to create new ones.

ACTIVITY

These scientists are in a laboratory working on an experiment.
Look carefully at the pictures. Can you spot the odd one out?

CHECK THE ANSWERS AT THE BACK OF THE BOOK!

OUR UNIVERSE

Our universe is everything we can touch, feel, sense, measure, and detect. It is made up of billions of galaxies, and it contains billions of stars. No one knows what shape the universe is, or how big it is, but we know it is vast because even using special instruments, we can't see the edge.

Objects that are bigger than a planet but smaller than a star are known as brown dwarfs. These are much cooler than stars, so they don't burn bright enough to be seen with the naked eye.

THE BIG BANG

The Big Bang theory states that about 13.7 billion years ago all the matter in the universe was concentrated into a single tiny point that rapidly expanded in a huge explosion.

Asteroids are rocky, airless worlds that orbit our sun. They are too small to be called planets. Scientists keep a close watch on asteroids that may pass close to Earth. These are called NEOs (Near-Earth Objects).

ACTIVITY

Can you place these objects found in space in order from the biggest to the smallest?

BIG

SMALL

BROWN DWARF
ASTEROID
STAR
GALAXY
PLANET
UNIVERSE

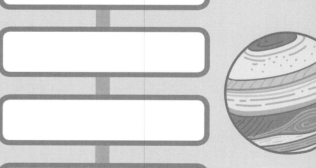

SPLENDID SPACE

Outer space begins around 60 miles (100 km) above Earth. It is a vacuum with no air, which means that sound cannot travel through it. If you were floating in space, no one could hear you talk, shout, or even scream!

IS SPACE BLACK?

Space only appears dark. Earth's atmosphere is full of particles that scatter light from the sun, creating a blue sky. But in space, the atmosphere does not contain enough particles and objects to scatter light.

ACTIVITY

The International Space Station (ISS) is an astronaut's home away from home. Draw arrows to insert the missing pieces from this picture of the ISS.

The ISS is the biggest object ever flown in space. It orbits Earth 16 times a day.

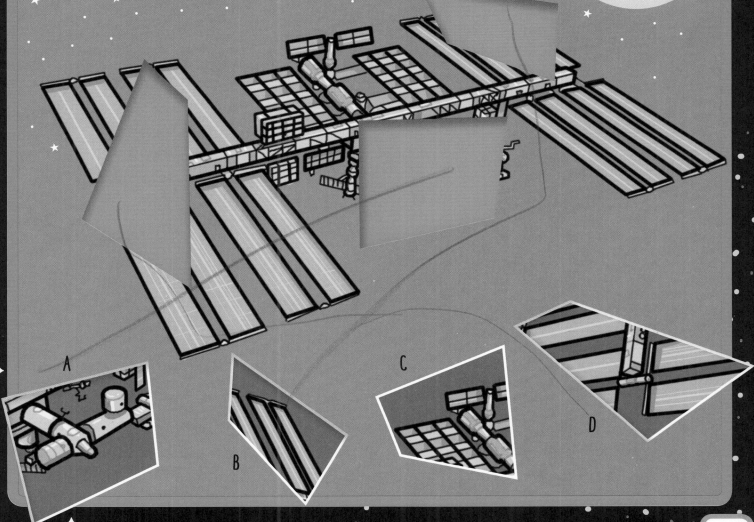

A

B

C

D

CHECK THE ANSWERS AT THE BACK OF THE BOOK!

THE SOLAR SYSTEM

For thousands of years, people thought the sun and the planets moved around Earth. Then astronomers proved that the sun was actually at the center. The solar system is made up of the sun, the eight planets, and everything else that revolves around it.

SUN

MERCURY
Closest to the sun

VENUS
The hottest planet in our solar system

EARTH
The only planet in our solar system to support life

MARS
Known as the "Red Planet" because of its red soil, which contains iron oxide (rust)

ACTIVITY

A mnemonic device is a saying that can help you remember the order of the planets. Each word in the saying begins with the same letter as the planet that you are trying to remember in order. **"My Very Excited Mother Just Served Us Nachos"** is an example of a mnemonic device.
Can you make up one of your own?

M ....

V ....

E ....

M ....

J ....

S ....

U ....

N ....

JUPITER

The largest planet; it has no solid surface

SATURN

Circled by rings made of ice and rock

URANUS

The only planet with a horizontal axis instead of a vertical axis, so it spins on its side

NEPTUNE

A cold planet with 13 moons

The sun won't last forever. Scientists have learned that it will continue to burn its hydrogen and helium fuel for another billion years, expanding to around a hundred times its current size and swallowing up all the planets in the solar system, including Earth.

EX-PLANET PLUTO

Until 2006, Pluto was known as the ninth planet from the sun, but it was demoted when the definition of a planet was changed. It is now known as a "dwarf planet."

ACTIVITY

We rely on the sun to survive. Without its light and heat, our planet would freeze and life on Earth would end. The sun is an enormous, 4.5-billion-year-old star that holds our solar system together.

Bring this flower to life by coloring it in.

MAGNIFICENT MOON

The moon is the brightest object in the sky, but it has no light of its own. It appears to shine because it reflects the light from the sun. The part of the moon facing away from the sun is in darkness.

The moon takes just over 27 days to orbit Earth. It is around 238,855 miles (384,400 km) away from our planet. If you were to travel there by car it would take around 130 days, driving at 80 mph (129 kmh).

ACTIVITY

As the moon travels around Earth, it looks as if it's changing shape in the sky. This is because we are seeing the moon lit up by the sun in different ways on different days.

Can you complete the rest of the lunar cycle? Color in the moons to show the portions that are in shade.

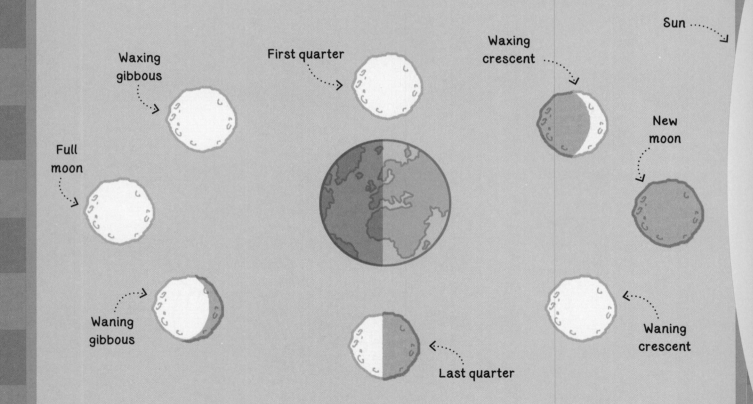

The moon rises and sets each day like the sun, but, unlike the sun, the moonrise and moonset times change as the moon moves through its cycle.

CHECK THE ANSWERS AT THE BACK OF THE BOOK!

THE STARS

There are at least a billion trillion stars in the universe. There are more stars than grains of sand on all of the beaches on Earth. Each star is a burning ball of gas that exists for billions of years.

NANCY GRACE ROMAN

Born in America in 1925, Nancy Roman organized a backyard astronomy club for her friends when she was just 11. She went on to become NASA's first chief of astronomy, helping develop amazing orbiting telescopes.

ACTIVITY

Connect the stars to create Canis Major—the Great Dog Constellation.

DID YOU KNOW?

Groups of stars that form a recognizable shape or pattern are known as constellations.

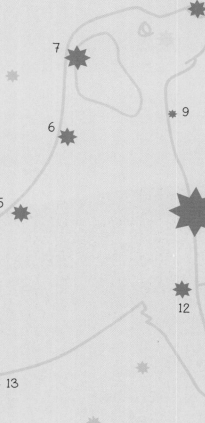
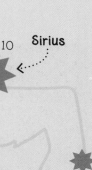

Sirius

LET THERE BE LIGHT

Light travels as waves and in straight lines. Objects don't give off their own light. It is the light bouncing off an object that allows us to see it.

When a ray of sunlight comes to Earth, the light seems white. In fact, it's made up of a spectrum of colors. A triangular block of glass called a prism can be used to split light into separate colors that we can see.

ACTIVITY

In nature, raindrops can refract white light into colors. Unscramble the letters to discover what we see when this happens.

B A N O W I R

....

Within this visible spectrum, the wavelength of light determines the color. For example, blue and green have shorter wavelengths than yellow, orange, and red.

Light travels much faster than sound, which is why we see lightning or fireworks explode before we hear them.

CHECK THE ANSWERS AT THE BACK OF THE BOOK!

A reflection is created when light is bounced off of a surface. If the surface is smooth, such as metal on the back of a mirror or a still pond, the reflection is sharp.

Use a pen to complete the boy's reflection in the mirror.

Optical sensors in fire alarms can detect ultraviolet rays in flames. They are often used for fire alarms in restaurants or homes.

ELECTRICITY

Electricity didn't have to be invented because it exists naturally in our world—it can be seen during thunderstorms when lightning bolts shoot down from the sky. Electricity that builds up in one place is called static electricity. Electricity that travels from one place to another is called current electricity.

Electricity is the flow of tiny particles called electrons. Each electron carries a tiny amount of electric charge. A bolt of lightning is caused by a buildup of electrons created by friction from ice crystals in a storm cloud.

THOMAS EDISON

Thomas Edison is often described as America's greatest inventor. In 1879, he invented the electric light bulb. The first bulb was an airtight glass container with a wire inside it.

In 1752, Benjamin Franklin wanted to prove that lightning was a form of electricity. He flew a kite during a thunderstorm and tied a metal key to a wet kite string to conduct the electricity. Electricity from the storm clouds flowed down the wet string and gave him a shock.

Franklin could have been badly hurt if his kite had been struck by lightning. This is not something you should ever try.

ACTIVITY

Complete each circuit by adding and naming the missing part.

An electrical circuit is a complete, unbroken path through which electricity can flow. Each circuit needs a switch, a power source (such as a battery), a load (such as a light bulb), and an uninterrupted pathway of wires between them.

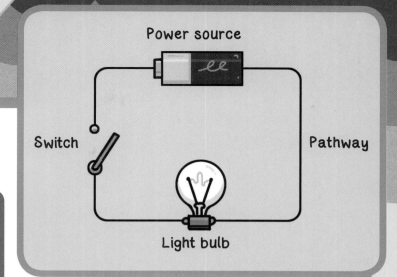

Power source

Switch

Pathway

Light bulb

A

What's broken?

Pathway

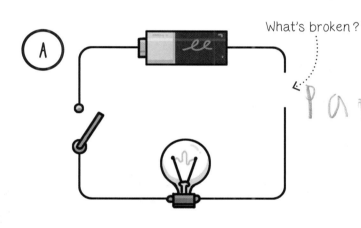

B

What's missing?

Power source

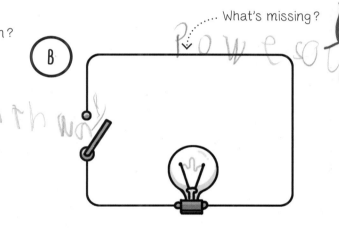

C

Switch

What's missing?

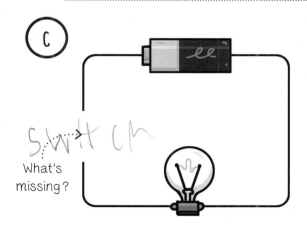

D

What's missing?

light bulb

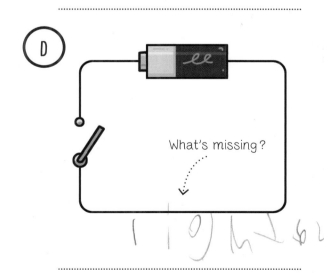

AMAZING X-RAYS

X-rays are a type of electromagnetic radiation. An X-ray's wavelength is smaller than that of an ultraviolet ray, which means that the human eye can't see it.

ACTIVITY

Color the shapes with an x in them black, to create an X-ray picture.

WILHELM RÖNTGEN

In 1895, Wilhelm Röntgen made a discovery that changed medical science. He found that some invisible rays could pass through the soft parts of a body to create a photographic image. He called them X-rays!

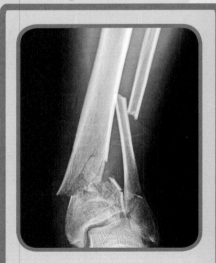

Doctors use X-ray pictures to check for broken bones. Airports use them to look for unsafe objects inside bags and suitcases.

CHECK THE ANSWERS AT THE BACK OF THE BOOK!

SOUND

Sound travels in waves. These invisible vibrations move through air, water, and solid objects and are then picked up by our ears. The size and shape of a sound wave will change the type of sound that we can hear.

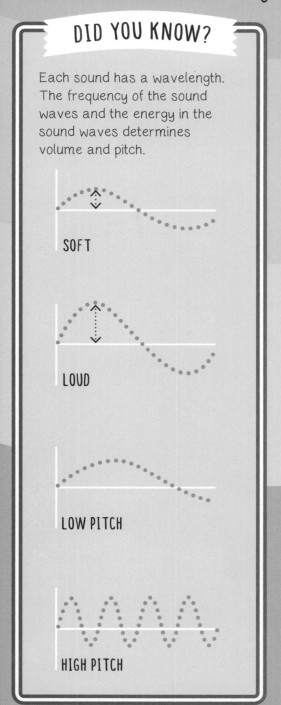

DID YOU KNOW?

Each sound has a wavelength. The frequency of the sound waves and the energy in the sound waves determines volume and pitch.

SOFT

LOUD

LOW PITCH

HIGH PITCH

ACTIVITY

Circle the sounds with short wavelengths.

MOUSE

OPERA SINGER

DOLPHIN

LION

WHISTLE

DRUM

TRACTOR

ALARM CLOCK

THUNDERSTORM

SEEING WITH SOUND

Bats and whales use sound to find their way around. Through a process called echolocation, they send out sounds that echo off the objects around them, letting them know where the objects are.

CHECK THE ANSWERS AT THE BACK OF THE BOOK!

ENERGY

In science, energy is described as the ability to do work. Everything needs energy to change and move, including living things. Energy is never created or destroyed—it is only changed from one state to another.

RENEWABLE VS. NONRENEWABLE

We get most of our energy from nonrenewable resources like fossil fuels, natural gas, coal, and uranium (a substance used to make electricity). Our planet only has a certain amount of these resources. Once they are used, they are gone.

Today, scientists are looking to harness new, renewable energy from natural resources that can be replenished and replaced, such as wind and fast-growing plants.

There are lots of different types of energy, and they all come from somewhere or something. The chemical energy that you use to move your body comes from the food you eat and the air you breathe. Outdoor heat energy comes from the sun.

Another problem with nonrenewable fossil fuels is that burning them pollutes our air with dangerous gases like carbon dioxide.

Read the clues, then unscramble the letters to find the renewable resources. The words you need are shown underneath the puzzle.

1 This power is from a burning star that Earth orbits.

ROSAL

_ _ _ _ _

2 Turbines on hills are used to capture this power.

NDIW

_ _ _ _

3 This resource is plant-based.

ODOW

_ _ _ _

4 This power comes from the movement of oceans and seas.

LITAD

_ _ _ _ _

WOOD   WIND   SOLAR   TIDAL

Electric cars do not use gasoline or nonrenewable energy. Tesla, an all-electric car, is named after the Serbian-American electrical engineer and physicist Nikola Tesla. Tesla invented the first alternating current motor.

HEAT

Heat energy is measured in joules. It is the result of the movements of tiny particles. These are always in motion, vibrating or bumping into each other. The motion of the particles creates a form of energy called heat that is present in all matter.

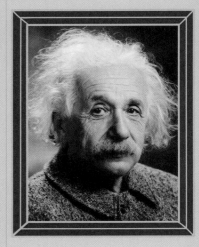

ALBERT EINSTEIN

Albert Einstein was one of the greatest scientists who ever lived. His groundbreaking theory of relativity, $E = mc^2$, proved that mass is another form of energy, just like heat or light.

ACTIVITY

Circle the objects that are conductors.

Conductors are materials that let heat pass easily through them. Insulators are materials that don't allow heat to pass easily through them.

FRYING PAN

RUBBER HOT WATER BOTTLE

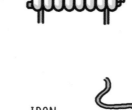

WOODEN DOOR

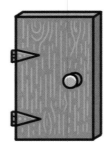

WOOL GLOVES

RADIATOR

METAL SPOON

PLASTIC WATER BOTTLE

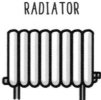

IRON

RING

CHECK THE ANSWERS AT THE BACK OF THE BOOK!

TEMPERATURE

Temperature is not the same as heat. Heat is the total amount of energy of all the molecules stored inside something. Temperature is a measurement of how hot or cold something is.

ACTIVITY

Temperature is measured in degrees Fahrenheit (°F) or Celsius (°C).
Color in the mercury in the thermometers to show each animal's body temperature.

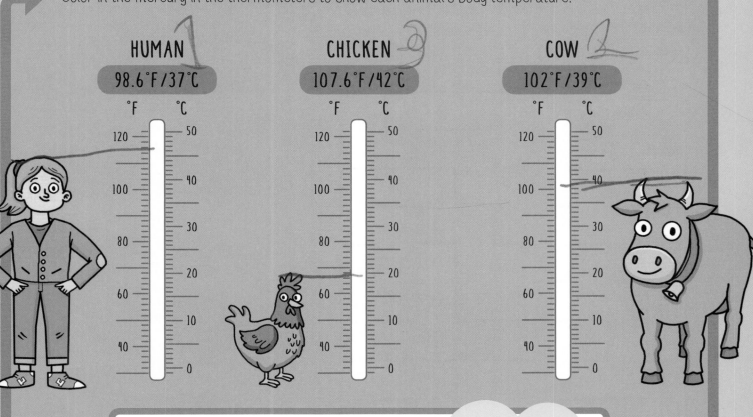

HUMAN
98.6°F / 37°C

CHICKEN
107.6°F / 42°C

COW
102°F / 39°C

Earth's average surface temperature has risen 33.9°F (1.1°C) since the late 19th century. This global warming is contributing to shrinking polar ice caps and warming oceans, putting many species of animals at risk and leading to extreme weather events.

CHECK THE ANSWERS AT THE BACK OF THE BOOK!

FABULOUS FORCES

You can't see it, but a force is a push or a pull. Adding force to an object by pushing or pulling results in motion. The physicist Isaac Newton described three Laws of Motion that explain how forces work on objects.

ACTIVITY

It takes force for this boy to push his shopping cart to the checkout. If he stops pushing, the cart will stop moving. Trace his path through the mini-maze.

FIRST LAW

An object at rest will stay at rest, and an object in motion will stay in motion with the same direction or speed unless acted upon by an external force.

When you are in a moving car, if the car brakes you will continue going forward (until the car comes to a stop or you are stopped by the force of the seatbelt).

SECOND LAW

The acceleration of an object is directly related to the strength of the force applied to it.

When we kick a ball, we exert force in a specific direction. The harder we kick the ball, the stronger the force applied to it and the farther it will travel.

THIRD LAW

For every action or force, there is an equal and opposite reaction or force.

When you sit on a chair, the chair needs to exert an equal force upward or the chair will collapse.

CHECK THE ANSWERS AT THE BACK OF THE BOOK!

Friction is a "grip-like" force that holds back the motion of a moving object. It happens wherever objects come into contact with each other. Friction in gases, such as pushing a paper airplane through air, is called air resistance or drag.

If you are running on pavement and want to stop, the friction between the soles of your shoes and the cement will help you stop more quickly. If you are running on a patch of ice, it would take longer to stop because the surface is smooth and there is less friction between the ice and your shoes.

ACTIVITY

Look at each picture. Decide whether it shows useful friction, too much friction, or not enough friction.

1 Emily has a ring stuck on her finger.

2 Maggie is striking a match.

3 Cole is rubbing his hands together to keep warm.

4 Carla is sledding.

5 A car is traveling on a road.

6 Sameer is slipping on ice.

USEFUL FRICTION   TOO MUCH FRICTION   NOT ENOUGH FRICTION

CHECK THE ANSWERS AT THE BACK OF THE BOOK!

GRAVITY

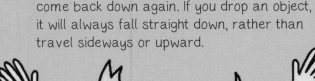

Gravity is a force by which a planet draws objects toward its center. Gravity holds our world and solar system together, keeping planets in orbit around the sun and the moon in orbit around Earth.

DID YOU KNOW?

Anything that has mass also has gravity. Objects with more mass have more gravity. This is why Jupiter, a larger planet, has a stronger gravitational pull than Earth. Mercury, a smaller planet, has a weaker gravitational pull.

Gravity is invisible, so how do we know it's there? If you jump in the air, you will always come back down again. If you drop an object, it will always fall straight down, rather than travel sideways or upward.

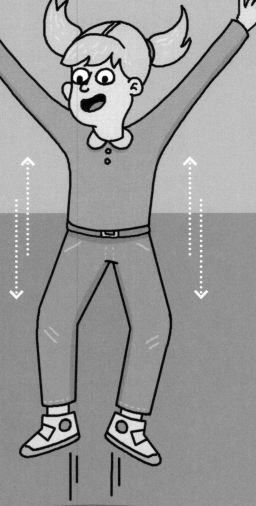

ISAAC NEWTON

English physicist, Sir Isaac Newton, first noted the existence of gravity when he saw an apple drop from a tree in his mother's garden.

The pull of gravity on an object is exactly the same as the weight of that object. This very heavy bowling ball has more gravity than a feather.

Very heavy bowling ball

Astronauts need special training to learn how to live in space, where they experience gravity differently. Before their mission, they ride NASA's "Vomit Comet," a specially fitted aircraft that simulates the feeling of weightlessness. They also practice underwater in a huge swimming pool called the Neutral Buoyancy Laboratory.

ACTIVITY

This astronaut is floating in zero gravity inside her space station. Spot and circle ten differences between the two images.

CHECK THE ANSWERS AT THE BACK OF THE BOOK!

MAGICAL MAGNETS

Magnetism is all about electrons—the tiny particles that whiz around the nucleus of an atom. Each electron behaves like a tiny magnet with a North and a South pole. When an atom's electrons are all lined up, pointing either north or south, it becomes magnetic.

Earth itself is a magnet. This is because its core is made of liquid nickel and iron. Earth rotates, making the liquid swirl around and generate a protective magnetic field around the planet.

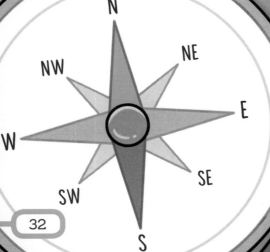

Earth has two North Poles and two South Poles. The geographic North and South Poles stay at the points where Earth's axis passes through the planet's surface. The magnetic North and South Poles occur wherever Earth's magnetic field points straight into and out of Earth at any given time.

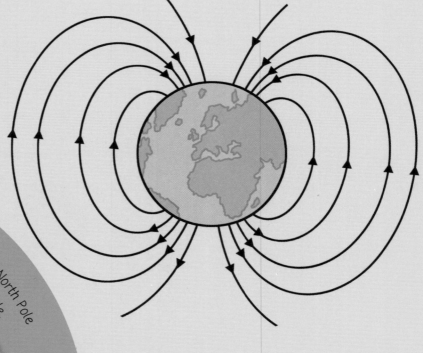

A compass aims toward the magnetic North Pole and not the geographic North Pole.

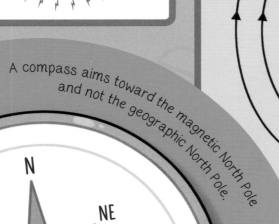

Sometimes Earth's magnetic field flips, so that it flows from north to south instead of south to north. Scientists don't yet understand why this happens.

ACTIVITY

Look at the panel of objects. Which objects would be
attracted to the magnet? Draw each one clinging to it.

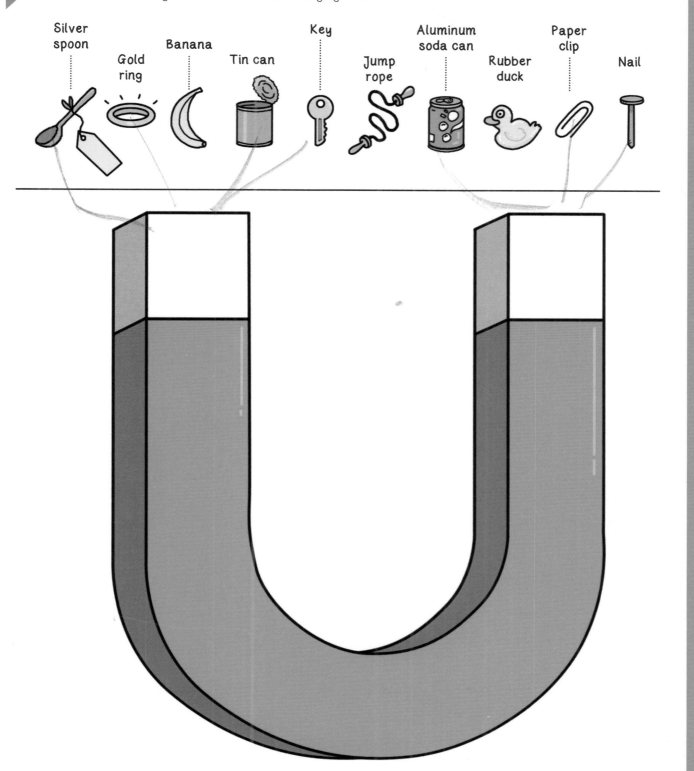

Silver spoon

Gold ring

Banana

Tin can

Key

Jump rope

Aluminum soda can

Rubber duck

Paper clip

Nail

CHECK THE ANSWERS AT THE BACK OF THE BOOK!

EXAMINING ELEMENTS

Everything in the universe is made up of elements. An element is a substance that can't be divided further into simpler substances. Our bodies are made up of three main elements. We are 65 percent oxygen, 18.5 percent carbon, and 9.5 percent hydrogen.

Elements are organized in a periodic table, which groups them according to how they behave. This helps scientists predict and explain how the elements will react with each other.

ACTIVITY

Unscramble the letters to reveal the elements that are commonly known metals. The pictures will help you!

1. NORI

2. NUMMIALU

3. RISLEV

4. LOGD

5. PERPOC

6. DALE

CHECK THE ANSWERS AT THE BACK OF THE BOOK!

AWESOME ATOMS

Atoms are the basic building blocks of matter. Everything is made up of atoms—you, this book, and your pencil or pen. Atoms join together to make molecules.

SAU LAN WU

Sau Lan Wu is a Chinese American particle physicist. She has dedicated her life to research on protons and neutrons. Her team first observed a tiny particle called the Higgs boson, which is thought to give all matter its mass.

ACTIVITY

A carbon atom has six protons, six neutrons, and six electrons. In this diagram of a carbon atom, color the protons blue, the neutrons red, and the electrons yellow. Remember, protons and neutrons are clustered in the center nucleus of the atom, and electrons spin around the nucleus.

Atoms are made up of smaller particles called protons, electrons, and neutrons. The same number of protons and neutrons cluster in the center of the atom called the nucleus. Electrons orbit the nucleus.

ELECTRON

PROTON

NEUTRON

STATES OF MATTER

Every material in the world exists in one of three states of matter. It must be either a solid, a liquid, or a gas. Changes in temperature or pressure can change the state of a substance.

HOW DOES THIS HAPPEN?

Atoms are never still. Even those in a solid object with a fixed shape vibrate back and forth. When you heat a solid, the atoms vibrate faster and faster and then move away from each other. They are still connected, but the bonds between them aren't strong enough to give the substance a fixed shape. When this happens, the substance turns from solid to liquid.

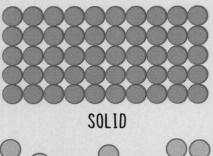

SOLID

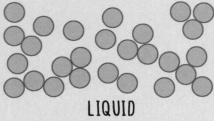

LIQUID

GAS

If you continue to heat the liquid, the bonds break and the atoms float away on their own. This happens when the liquid turns to gas.

ACTIVITY

Draw circles to represent how compact the atoms are for substances in these three different states—solid, liquid, or gas.

Both cooling and heating can change the state of a substance. For example, if you place water in a freezer, it freezes into a solid. But if you leave an ice cube in warm temperatures, it melts to become a liquid.

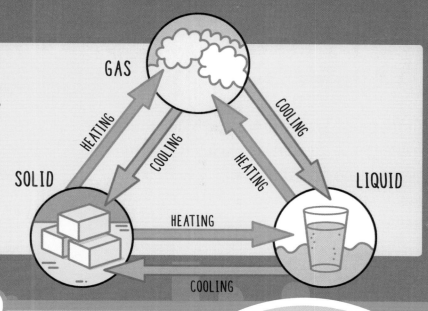

GAS

HEATING

COOLING

COOLING

HEATING

SOLID

HEATING

LIQUID

COOLING

ACTIVITY

Find a solid, a liquid, and a gas in each picture. Label it with "S" for solid, "L" for liquid, or "G" for gas.

1

2

3

MARVELOUS MIXTURES

Many common substances are actually mixtures of other ingredients. A mixture is made from different substances that are not chemically joined and can be easily separated from each other. Sugar dissolved in tea is an example of a mixture.

Some substances, such as oil and water or wax and water, don't mix. A suspension of two liquids that doesn't mix is called an emulsion. Have you ever seen a lava lamp? The lamp heats the wax, which melts and moves around in the water, never mixing with it.

ACTIVITY

Look at the labels, then draw some colorful emulsions inside these lava lamps.

Red water
Yellow wax

Blue water
White wax

Purple water
Red wax

Green water
Blue wax

CHEMICAL REACTIONS

Chemical reactions happen when two or more molecules interact and join together to make a new substance. Many chemical reactions can only start when the ingredients are heated. Some reactions are permanent and some are reversible.

We rely on many chemical reactions in everyday life.

A chemical reaction called photosynthesis is used by plants to convert carbon dioxide and water into food (glucose) and oxygen.

Thousands of chemical reactions take place as we digest our food. Saliva and stomach acid create chemical reactions that break down food.

Respiration is the chemical reaction by which our bodies release energy for use in our daily lives. It allows us to move, grow, and repair cells.

ACTIVITY

Which of these is NOT a chemical reaction?

A — A rusting key

B — A burning log

C — A meowing cat

D — An egg cooking

ACIDS AND BASES

Acids are common in nature. Lemon juice contains citric acid, which makes it taste sour, and it stings if we accidentally squirt it in our eyes. A nettle plant sting is caused by tiny amounts of acid that get transferred to our skin from the leaves.

Any chemical you come across can be acidic or basic. The strength of an acid or base is measured using the pH scale, which involves calculating the number of hydrogen ions in a substance. Strong base substances like bleach have a pH of 13 or 14, because they have few hydrogen ions. Strong acids, such as stomach acid, have a pH of 1 because they have a lot of hydrogen ions.

ACTIVITY

Draw the missing icons to represent each item on the pH scale.

STOMACH ACID

LEMON

GRAPES

TOMATOES

BANANAS

MILK

0   1   2   3   4   5   6

Acids are also common in our bodies. Our stomachs contain a very strong acid to help us digest food. You may also have felt the buildup of lactic acid after exercise. It creates a burning sensation in tired muscles.

Chemical reactions involving acids and bases can be useful. Soap is made by an acid–base reaction between fatty acids and a strong base.

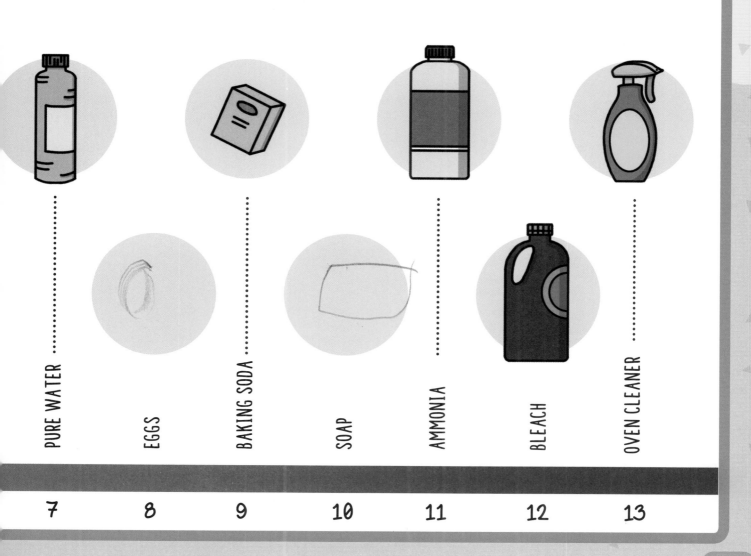

PURE WATER

EGGS

BAKING SODA

SOAP

AMMONIA

BLEACH

OVEN CLEANER

7   8   9   10   11   12   13

PLANT LIFE

Plants are vital to life on Earth. They help regulate the water cycle, form the habitats of many animals, give us food, and produce the oxygen that we breathe.

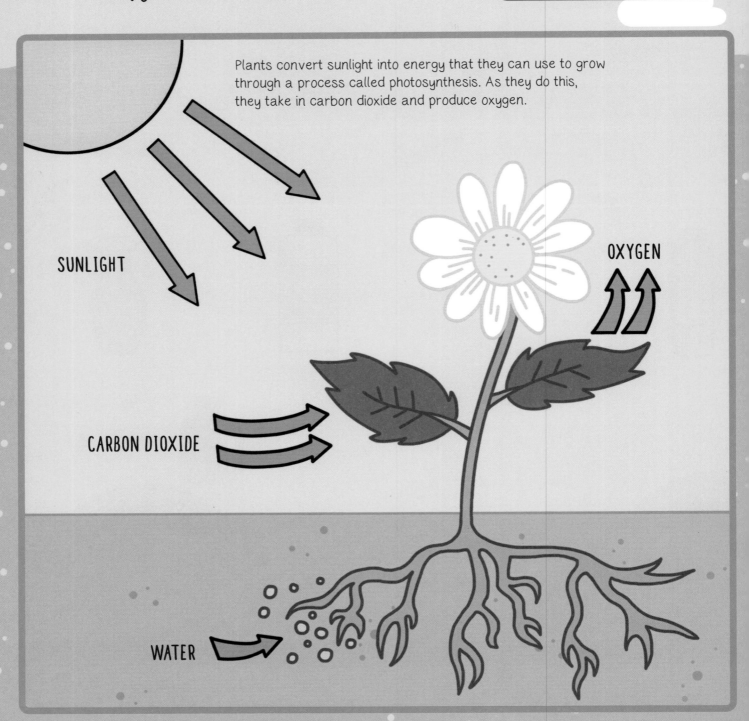

Plants convert sunlight into energy that they can use to grow through a process called photosynthesis. As they do this, they take in carbon dioxide and produce oxygen.

SUNLIGHT

OXYGEN

CARBON DIOXIDE

WATER

Plants are smarter than you might think. Through natural selection, plants have evolved, developing tricks to make sure their species survive.

❀ Some plants have pods that explode when they're ripe, shooting out the seeds.

❀ Some seeds have hooks to hitchhike on the bodies of birds and bees. Others are in tasty fruit that gets eaten, and then pass through the animal undamaged to land on fertile ground to grow.

❀ Some seeds have parachutes or wings to catch the wind and fly to new, rich environments.

ACTIVITY

Which of these bees will pollinate the pink flower on the way to the red one? Trace back the trails!

Pollen is a form of plant seed that needs to be transferred from the male flower to the female flower. Bees are great pollinators. They spread pollen that gets caught in their hair as they travel from flower to flower.

CHECK THE ANSWERS AT THE BACK OF THE BOOK!

ANIMAL LIFE

Our planet is full of life, but exactly how many species of animal exist? To date, around 2 million species have been identified, but researchers believe the actual number, including insects, may lie anywhere between 100 million and 2 billion.

Some species on Earth are hanging by a thread. When a species is wiped out, it is called extinction. The Bornean orangutan, the giant tusked bull elephant, and the eastern lowland gorilla are all critically endangered (near extinction)

ACTIVITY

The number of wild animals living on Earth is falling every year. Follow the lines to match each of these creatures with its conservation status.

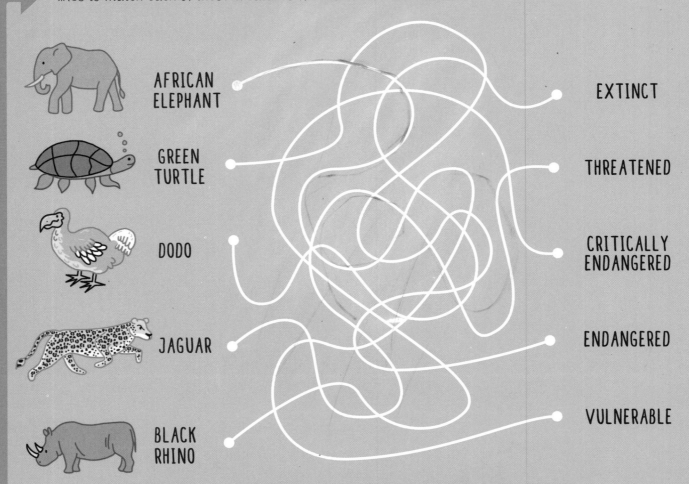

AFRICAN ELEPHANT

GREEN TURTLE

DODO

JAGUAR

BLACK RHINO

EXTINCT

THREATENED

CRITICALLY ENDANGERED

ENDANGERED

VULNERABLE

A major study released by the World Wildlife Fund revealed that the number of wild animals living on Earth is set to fall two-thirds by 2020. Human activities are all to blame, such as the destruction of wild habitats, hunting, and pollution.

CHECK THE ANSWERS AT THE BACK OF THE BOOK!

Humans have learned to take inspiration from animals and the natural world. Using certain aspects of the way animals look or function for our own purposes is called biomimicry.

ACTIVITY

Can you match each example from the natural world to the human invention it inspired?

 1   **Humpback whale's flipper**

 2   **Shark skin**

 3   **Spider's silk web**

4   **Iridescent butterfly wings**

 5      **Burrs on a dog's fur**

6   **Kingfisher's beak**

A   **E-READER SCREEN**

B   **VELCRO**

C   **WIND TURBINE**

D   **JAPANESE BULLET TRAIN**

E   **SWIMSUIT**

F   **MEDICAL TAPE**

CHECK THE ANSWERS AT THE BACK OF THE BOOK!

OUR BRILLIANT BODIES

The human body is amazing. It is a collection of cells and muscles held together by a bony skeleton and is made of about 7 octillion atoms. An octillion is the same as a billion billion billion!

Your body needs energy to survive. It gets that energy from digesting the food that you chew and swallow. Stomach acids break down the food, passing nutrients to the bloodstream. Blood carries those nutrients, plus oxygen, to the body's cells where they are converted to energy.

BODY FACTS

Your pinky provides half of your hand strength, while your big toes help you balance.

Your nose can smell 1 trillion different scents.

Your heart beats around one hundred thousand times a day, pumping 5.5 liters of blood per minute.

Your skin's outer layer sheds every two to four weeks.

Your skeleton is very important. It protects internal organs like the heart, lungs, and liver. A baby is usually born with 270 bones, but over the years some bones fuse together. An adult skeleton only has 206 bones.

ACTIVITY

Use the color copy grid to draw your own skeleton.

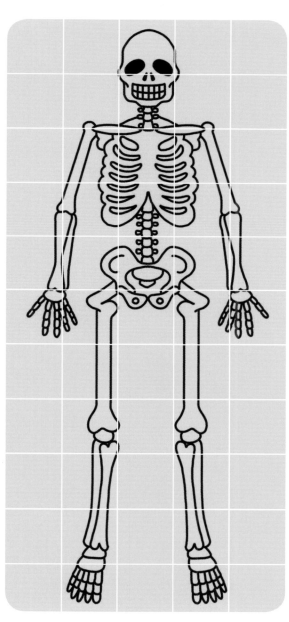

Can you locate...

THE CRANIUM   **THE RIBS**   **THE PELVIS**   **THE PHALANGES**   **THE FEMUR**

CHECK THE ANSWERS AT THE BACK OF THE BOOK!

CELLS

Cells are the building blocks that make up all living things, including the human body. We have over 10 trillion cells in our bodies. Cells provide structure for the body, take nutrients from food, and convert nutrients into energy.

Cells are specialized, which means that different cells have different jobs.

• Nerve cells transmit information between parts of the body using electrical and chemical signals.

• White blood cells help defend the body against infectious disease and foreign bodies.

ACTIVITY

Human and plant cells have some similarities and some differences. Look at the cells carefully. Record the qualities that are the same in the SIMILAR column in the table below. Record any unique structures under DIFFERENCES. Write an "A" or a "P" after each entry to show whether it is an ANIMAL or a PLANT.

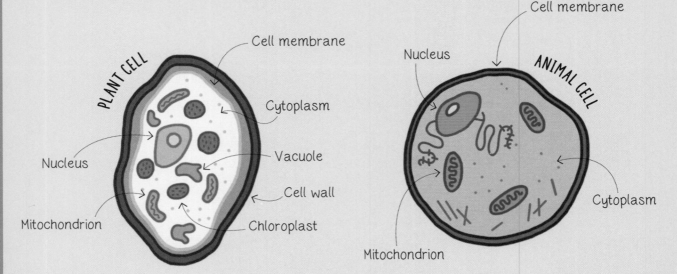

SIMILARITIES		DIFFERENCES	

CHECK THE ANSWERS AT THE BACK OF THE BOOK!

BREATHING AND CIRCULATION

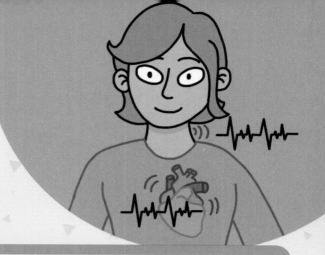

When you breathe, you draw oxygen from the air into your lungs in a process called inhalation. This oxygen is carried through your body in your bloodstream.

ACTIVITY

You can use your pulse to track your heart rate. To locate your pulse, use the two fingers closest to your thumb and place them on the underside of the wrist of your other hand.

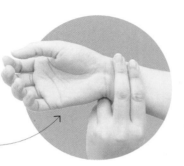

Your beating heart pushes so much blood through your body that you can feel a little thud in the arteries closest to the skin every time your heart beats. This is your pulse.

Count how many times you feel your pulse in 60 seconds. This is your resting heart rate. Then do the same after exercise. Record your findings. What do you notice?

MY RESTING HEART RATE IS:

MY HEART RATE AFTER 10 JUMPS:

MY HEART RATE AFTER 20 JUMPS:

MY HEART RATE AFTER 30 JUMPS:

These results show that:

GENETICS

Every cell in the human body contains genes. Genes have special codes that give you certain traits, which are features that are passed on to you—or inherited—from your parents.

ACTIVITY

Finish coloring the double helix to show the repeating pattern that is found in DNA. The pattern has been started for you.

Genes are short sections of a molecule called DNA (deoxyribonucleic acid). DNA is made up of base pairs that always match in the same pattern.

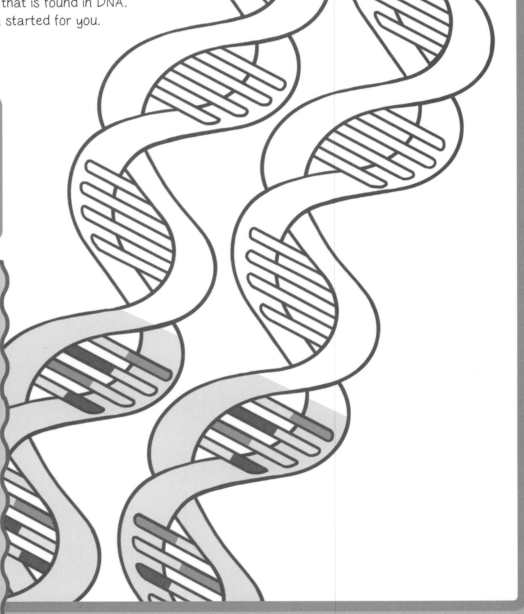

ROSALIND FRANKLIN

This English scientist took X-rays of DNA, which led directly to the discovery of its amazing structure. Sadly, Franklin died in 1958 before the structure was discovered.

The DNA molecule looks like a spiral staircase called a double helix. It is made up of two long strands twisted around each other. DNA molecules carry the genetic code that makes you unique.

FOOD CHAINS

Food chains and webs show where energy begins and how it is transferred through an ecosystem to animals and humans. Energy is transferred through consumption (eating). Food webs show all the possible paths that energy can take.

The sun is the source of all natural energy on our planet, so every chain starts with it. The sun also lies at the center of all food webs.

Carnivores are meat eaters, while herbivores eat plants. Humans are omnivores. Omnivores eat meat and plants, including fruits and vegetables. Humans and large wild predators sit at the top of food chains. Under them are smaller carnivores, then herbivores.

ACTIVITY

Draw these plants and animals in the correct order (and label them) to create a food chain that starts with the sun and ends with the largest energy consumer.

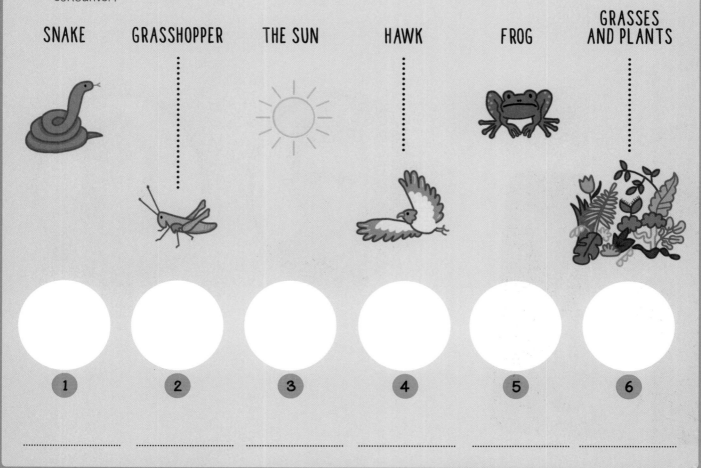

SNAKE   GRASSHOPPER   THE SUN   HAWK   FROG   GRASSES AND PLANTS

1   2   3   4   5   6

CHECK THE ANSWERS AT THE BACK OF THE BOOK!

MEDICINE

In the Middle Ages, people usually only lived until they were around 45 years old. Today, the average human life span has reached 71 years. Many amazing scientific discoveries have occurred over the centuries, allowing us to live longer and healthier lives.

Today, our health depends on both great advances in medicine that are from the past and cutting-edge new discoveries.

PAST MEDICAL ADVANCES

- Penicillin
- Anesthesia
- Germ theory
- Vaccines

MODERN DISCOVERIES

- Robotic prosthetics
- Robotic surgery
- Organ transplants
- Nuclear medicine

WOMEN IN SCIENCE

Female scientists have been equally influential in the field of medicine. **Marie Curie** was a Polish physicist known for her work on radioactivity. **Jane Cooke Wright** was an oncologist working in the field of chemotherapy. **Alice Ball**, an African American chemist, developed the only successful treatment for leprosy until antibiotics came along.

There are lots of amazing young women today, too. **Molly Stevens** is a Professor of Biomedical Materials and Regenerative Medicine in England. Her research could help fix failing organs in very young children.

MARIE CURIE

MOLLY STEVENS

Nuclear medicine is a new branch of imaging that uses tiny amounts of radioactive material to diagnose and determine the severity of diseases, such as cancer and heart disease. It is painless and doesn't involve surgery.

ACTIVITY

Medicine involves many specialized fields. Find the icon that illustrates what these medical professionals do.

1.
CARDIOLOGIST

2.
PEDIATRICIAN

3.
RADIOLOGIST

4.
NEUROLOGIST

5.
OPHTHALMOLOGIST

6.
ORTHOPEDIST

A

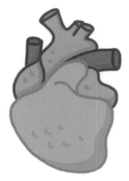

B

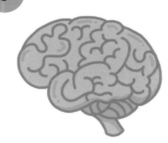

C

....

D

E

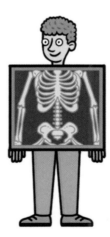

F

....

EARTH

Earth is the shape of a slightly squashed sphere. It spins on its axis—an imaginary line through the center of Earth that runs from the North Pole down to the South Pole. Earth is known as the Goldilocks planet because it has conditions which are "neither too hot, too cold, but just right" to support life.

Earth spins around once every 24 hours. As Earth turns, the area facing the sun experiences "day," while the part that's facing away from the sun experiences "night."

Earth's rotation is gradually slowing, but it's happening so slowly that it could be 140 years before the length of its rotation increases to 25 hours.

If you cut Earth in half, you would see it is made up of four layers. The thin, rocky outer layer is called the crust. Below this is the mantle—the widest section of Earth. Next comes the outer core, made up of liquid nickel and iron. The center of Earth is called the inner core. It is the hottest part of the planet.

ACTIVITY

Label each layer of Earth shown in this picture.

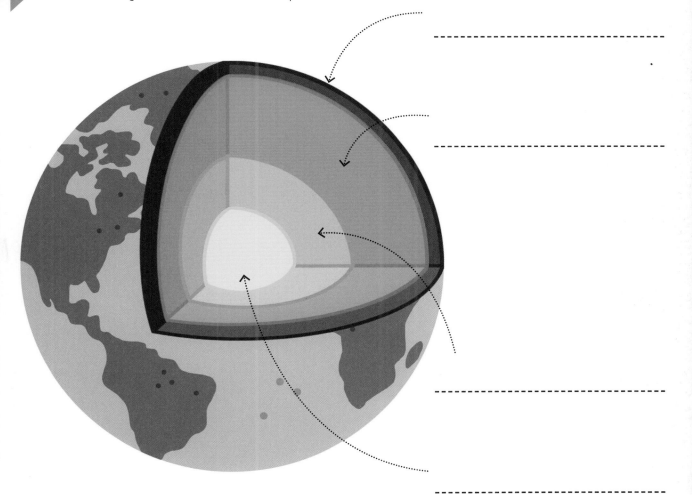

CRUST   MANTLE   INNER CORE   OUTER CORE

SHIFTING GROUND

Earth's crust is like a jigsaw puzzle. It is made up of interlocking pieces called tectonic plates. These plates are not fixed. Instead, they float on a layer of hot liquid rock known as magma.

When tectonic plates slide over and under one another, it forces the magma upward. The magma becomes lava as it bursts out of Earth's surface in a volcanic eruption.

ACTIVITY

Grab a red pen or pencil, and make this volcano erupt. Show the magma shooting up from the magma chamber and out of the volcano's crater. Add the correct words to complete the labeled diagram.

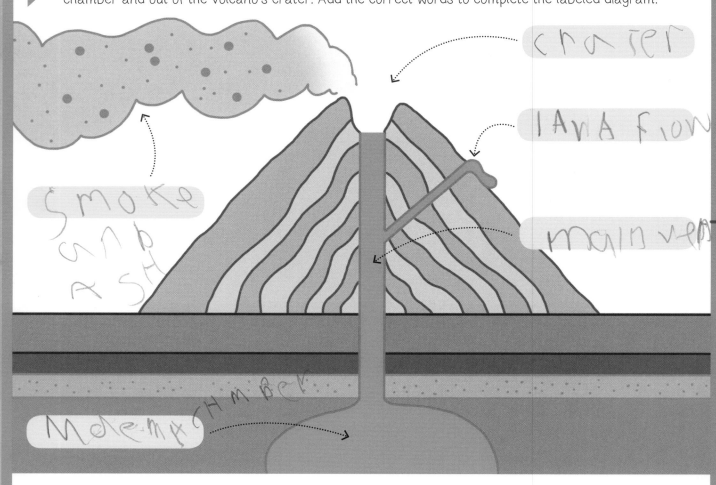

crater

lAvA Fiow

main vent

Smoke and ASH

Mole-mAcHmBeR

CRATER   LAVA FLOW

MAGMA CHAMBER   SMOKE AND ASH   MAIN VENT

CHECK THE ANSWERS AT THE BACK OF THE BOOK!

ROCKS AND FOSSILS

Studying rocks found on Earth's surface allows scientists, called geologists, to answer lots of important questions about our world.

ANNA K. BEHRENSMEYER

For almost 30 years, U.S. scientist Anna K. Behrensmeyer has been engaged in geological field research in Kenya. She is a world leader in the study of fossil records and what they can tell us about the past.

HOW OLD IS EARTH?

Geologists have found rocks dating back over 4 million years and can date Earth to be 4.5 million years old.

WAS THERE LIFE ON EARTH BEFORE MAN?

Yes. We know this through the discovery of fossils that were formed when ancient plants and animals died and became trapped inside deposits of sand or mud. Over time, these deposits then turned to rock and left a record of ancient life forms.

ACTIVITY

We have a long history of studying fossils, and we're still making new discoveries today! Can you locate these four key fossil findings on the world map and write the continent name in the box below?

EUROPE

ASIA

NORTH AMERICA

AFRICA

SOUTH AMERICA

AUSTRALIA

1. **Velociraptor and Protoceratops in combat**
Discovered: Gobi Desert, Mongolia. Date: 1971

2. **Herbivore Muttaburrasaurus**
Discovered: Muttaburra, Queensland, Australia.
Date: 1963

3. **Archaeopteryx skeleton**
Discovered: Solnhofen, Germany.
Date: 1860

4. **Gigantic Titanosaur bones**
Discovered: Patagonia, Argentina.
Date: 2014

CHECK THE ANSWERS AT THE BACK OF THE BOOK!

WONDERFUL WATER

Earth is unique in our solar system because of one precious, life-giving substance—water. A massive 71 percent of Earth's surface is made up of water. Earth's oceans help regulate its climate, absorbing heat in the summer and releasing it in the winter.

WE DEPEND ON CLEAN WATER:

1. FOR OUR BODIES TO FUNCTION.

2. TO GROW CROPS.

3. TO WASH OUR FOOD AND BODIES.

ACTIVITY

Estimates vary, but the average person uses around 40 gallons (150 liters) of water a day.

Complete the table to figure out how much water you use in a week.

ACTIVITY	MEASUREMENT	NUMBER OF TIMES	USAGE PER ACTIVITY
Taking a bath	21 gallons (80 liters)		
Taking a shower	11 gallons (45 liters)		
Brushing my teeth	1.5 gallons (6 liters)		
Washing my hands/face	1.5 gallons (6 liters)		
Drinking water	8 ounces (225 milliliters)		
Using the dishwasher	4 gallons (15 liters)		
Flushing the toilet	2.5 gallons (9 liters)		
		TOTAL USAGE	

Multiply the number of gallons by the number of times you've done an activity to get the total usage for that activity. Add the **USAGE PER ACTIVITY** figures to get the total water usage.

Earth has five main oceans—the Atlantic, the Arctic, the Indian, the Pacific, and the Southern Oceans. Together, these contain the greatest diversity of life on our planet.

THE WATER CYCLE

Most of the world's water is collected in the oceans, but it doesn't stay there. Through a chemical process known as the water cycle, water changes its state of matter and goes from land to sky and back again.

Water on Earth's surface in oceans, lakes, or rivers turns from a liquid to a gas and becomes water vapor. This is known as evaporation. The vapor rises and cools, then turns back into a liquid, forming clouds. This is called condensation. When water droplets become too heavy for a cloud to hold them, they fall to the ground as rain. This is called precipitation.

A raindrop can take between two and seven minutes to reach the ground.

ACTIVITY

Starting with evaporation, add arrows pointing in the right direction to show each step in the water cycle.

CONDENSATION

EVAPORATION

PRECIPITATION

CHECK THE ANSWERS AT THE BACK OF THE BOOK!

THE FUTURE OF SCIENCE

Exciting new discoveries are happening all over the world, all the time. Right now, scientists are asking themselves fascinating questions. What worlds are left to be explored? Which past discoveries need re-examining? What will we invent next?

These are all questions for the future of science—a future that starts with you!

ACTIVITY

Use this laboratory page to brainstorm solutions to one of the problems below:

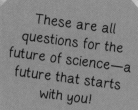

1 Our Earth's atmosphere is getting hotter due to climate change. How can we change cars to use less gas?

_____

_____

_____

_____

2 It will take years for a rocket to get to Mars. How will the astronauts eat?

_____

_____

_____

_____

3 Earth's fossil fuels will not last forever. How can we get more energy from the sun?

_____

_____

_____

_____

THE BIG SCIENCE QUIZ

Now it's time to test your science skills! Check the right answers. Look back through the book if you need to check your facts.

1

STEM stands for...

a) Science, time, engineering, and machinery ☐

b) Space, time, elements, and machinery ☐

c) Science, technology, engineering, and math ☐

2

Physics is the study of...

a) Living things ☐

b) Energy and forces ☐

c) Substances that make up matter ☐

3

The inventor who said "Eureka!" in his bathtub was...

a) Aristotle ☐   b) Archimedes ☐   c) Anning ☐

4

What percentage of the Earth's surface is made up of water?

a) 71 percent ☐

b) 53 percent ☐

c) 45 percent ☐

5

The shape of a DNA molecule is also known as a...

a) Double helix ☐

b) Double hexagon ☐

c) Double heptagon ☐

6

The theory explaining the way the universe was formed is called...

a) The Brown Dwarf ☐

b) The Big Bang ☐

c) The Black Hole ☐

CHECK THE ANSWERS AT THE BACK OF THE BOOK!

7 The adult human skeleton usually has...

a) 106 bones ☐

b) 270 bones ☐

c) 206 bones ☐

8 You would use a prism to...

a) Split white light into a spectrum of colored light ☐

b) See the edge of the observable universe ☐

c) Split an atom ☐

9 Electricity can be described as...

a) The flow of tiny particles called electrons ☐

b) The flow of tiny particles called molecules ☐

c) The flow of tiny particles called protons ☐

10 Earth is made up of...

a) Tectonic plates ☐   b) Magma plates ☐   c) Sedimentary plates ☐

11 Plants change sunlight into energy for growth using...

a) Respiration ☐

b) Photosynthesis ☐

c) Sublimation ☐

12

1 1.008
H
Hydrogen

4 9.012
Be
Beryllium

6 12.011
C
Carbon

3 6.941
Li
Lithium

5 10.811
B
Boron

The scale used to measure the acidity of a substance is...

a) The pH scale ☐

b) The Fahrenheit scale ☐

c) The periodic scale of elements ☐

CHECK THE ANSWERS AT THE BACK OF THE BOOK!

ANSWERS

Page 8
FIELDS OF SCIENCE
1. G   2. D   3. F   4. B   5. H   6. E   7. C   8. A

Page 9
THE HISTORY OF SCIENCE
Archimedes said "**Eureka!**". It means, "I have it!"

Page 11
THINK LIKE A SCIENTIST
The answer is B. The yellow flask is a different shape.

Page 12
OUR UNIVERSE

BIG
UNIVERSE
GALAXY
STAR
BROWN DWARF
PLANET
ASTEROID
SMALL

Page 13
SPLENDID SPACE
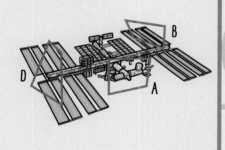

Page 16
MAGNIFICENT MOON
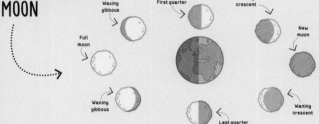

Page 18
LET THERE BE LIGHT
A spectrum of light that happens when sunlight is refracted through raindrops is a **RAINBOW**.

Page 21
ELECTRICITY
The missing elements in each circuit are:

A. Broken pathway
B. Power source (battery)
C. Switch
D. Load (light bulb)

Page 22
AMAZING X-RAYS

Page 23
SOUND

Page 25
ENERGY
1. Solar   2. Wind   3. Wood   4. Tidal

Page 26
HEAT
The conductors are:
Frying pan / Radiator / Ring / Metal spoon / Iron

Page 27
TEMPERATURE
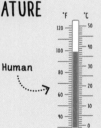
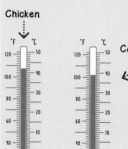

Human — Chicken — Cow

Pages 28-29
FABULOUS FORCES

USEFUL FRICTION
- Sledding
- Rubbing hands to keep warm
- Striking a match
- Car tires on a road

TOO MUCH FRICTION
- A ring stuck on a finger

NOT ENOUGH FRICTION
- Slipping on the ice

Page 31
GRAVITY

Page 33
MAGICAL MAGNETS
A tin can, a paper clip, and a nail would be attracted to the magnet.

Page 34
EXAMINING ELEMENTS
1. Iron   2. Aluminum   3. Silver   4. Gold
5. Copper   6. Lead

Pages 36–37
STATES OF MATTER

1. Solid—the car
   Liquid—gasoline
   Gas—exhaust vapor

2. Solid—the basket
   Liquid—water in the lake
   Gas—helium inside the balloon

3. Gas—air in the beach ball
   Liquid—water in the rock pool
   Solid—the beach chair

Page 39
CHEMICAL REACTIONS
The answer is C. A meowing cat is not a chemical reaction.

Page 43
PLANT LIFE

Pages 44–45
ANIMAL LIFE
African elephant .... VULNERABLE
Green turtle .... ENDANGERED
Dodo .... EXTINCT
Jaguar .... THREATENED
Black rhino .... CRITICALLY ENDANGERED

1. C   2. E   3. F
4. A   5. B   6. D

Page 47
OUR BRILLIANT BODIES

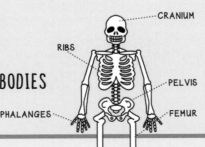

Page 48
CELLS
Plant and animal cells both have a cell membrane, cytoplasm, nucleus, and mitochondrion. The plant cell has a cell wall, vacuole, and chloroplast.

Page 51
FOOD CHAINS
1. Sun   2. Grasses and plants   3. Grasshopper
4. Frog   5. Snake   6. Hawk

Page 53
MEDICINE
1. A   2. F   3. E   4. B   5. C   6. D

Page 55
EARTH

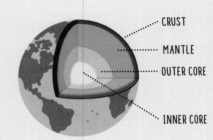

Page 56
SHIFTING GROUND

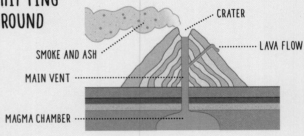

Page 57
ROCKS AND FOSSILS
1. Asia 2. Australia 3. Europe 4. South America

Page 59
THE WATER CYCLE

Pages 61–62
THE BIG SCIENCE QUIZ
1. c   2. b   3. b   4. a   5. a   6. b
7. c   8. a   9. a   10. a   11. b   12. a